MW01127374

Heavenly Paws

A Beloved Dog Is Reborn

By: Lynda J. Austin

authorHOUSE™

1663 LIBERTY DRIVE, SUITE 200
BLOOMINGTON, INDIANA 47403
(800) 839-8640
WWW.AUTHORHOUSE.COM

This book is meant to be thought provoking. The subject of my dog reincarnating is true to the best of my knowledge. It is based on my research and my own opinions and beliefs. Each reader should come to their own conclusion.

First published by AuthorHouse 05/25/05

ISBN: 1-4208-3370-7 (sc)
ISBN: 1-4208-3371-5 (dj)

Library of Congress Control Number: 2005902068

Printed in the United States of America
Bloomington, Indiana

This book is printed on acid-free paper.

Dedicated

I dedicate this book to the three exemplary veterinarians who took extraordinary care of my dogs – Jack Burke, DVM, Jeffrey Stuppler, DVM, and Henry Randazzo, DVM. All of these dedicated doctors unselfishly make themselves available for emergencies after hours.

Acknowledgments

First of all, I thank all of my precious dogs who have taught me about life – Misty, Maxwell, Melody, Gabriel, Gunther, and my reincarnation Max-Jacob. I cannot even begin to imagine what life would have been without them.

My editor Steve Covington offered his expertise and encouragement. I thank him for his help.

I want to thank my grandfather for teaching me to love and respect animals. I thank my parents for giving me my first miniature schnauzer named Misty. Thanks to my husband for the gift of Max and Melody. I thank my breeder for Gabbie and her help in finding my reincarnated Maxwell.

Thank you to my psychic Regina Becker for helping me connect with Maxwell.

Table of Contents

INTRODUCTION

This book is a collection of stories based on my special memories of my dogs.

The book also deals with what I believe is the reincarnation of my dog named Max. All my dogs were individually special, but Max had a particularly strong bond with me. I always tell people we were each others "heart light". Losing Max and having him return to me has taught me to handle my grief over the other losses in my life. It has taught me exactly how loving the Universe is. I have learned that life is a continual transition. We should look to the leaves falling, the buds sprouting, and the leaves appearing once again. Nature is God's whisper to us, and holds the answers. We simply have to look in the right places.

Section One

[Max and Melody]

HOW TO BE A CHAMPION PET

1. Look sad when your mistress or master leaves the house.
2. Guard the house when your mistress or master is away.
3. Answer the telephone when it rings.
4. Watch for the man in the truck who steals the garbage.
5. Eye that man who comes in the brown truck and throws boxes on the porch.
6. Watch for the driver in the yellow bus taking the neighbor children away.
7. Look for signs of rain or snow.
8. Listen for thunder and warn the mistress or master of the house.
9. Watch for your mistress and master to come home.
10. Enthusiastically greet your mistress and man of the house, jumping up and down and kissing them.
11. Check all packages for food or toys.
12. Watch for chipmunks, squirrels, birds, rabbits, deer, and the occasional reptile.
13. Sleep on your mistress' lap.
14. At outdoor cafes sit and behave.
15. Bark at the gas station.
16. Shake hands with everyone you meet.
17. Hold hands with people when meeting them to show warmth.
18. Lick the human's tears away.

WHAT MY DOGS HAVE TAUGHT ME

The stories in this book are memories of my champion pets. They are simple memories, but they are significant because of their simplicity. My dogs have not only been a source of unconditional love, but also a source of wisdom. I believe animals were put on Earth for mankind to learn from. Dogs function by instinct and they have outstanding qualities. Dog's endearing qualities of unconditional love, trust, and forgiveness are qualities most of mankind needs to strive for.

Our dogs greet us at the door ecstatically joyful each time we come home. No matter how many times we come home in a day they are just as happy. My dogs watched for me to come home with their noses pressed up against the window.

I believe the divorce rate would drop substantially if we treated our spouses with the same joyfulness as our dog companions. Our dogs don't judge us in any way. They don't care how big our house is, what kind of car we drive, how much money we have, where we went to school, if we are good looking, or how much we weigh. Our faithful companions are non-judgmental.

Can you imagine how much healthier our society would be if it were nonjudgmental.

Dogs are not by nature mean. People make dogs mean either by irresponsible breeding, or by abuse. Again, we can look at this and learn from the dogs. We still live in a country with an over population of dogs. They become homeless because of irresponsible people. Dogs should be spayed or neutered. Breeding should only be done by knowledgeable people with a concern of eradicating known health problems.

Dogs that are abused may become aggressive, making it impossible to place them in a home. Again, if we examine this, the same thing is happening to children in our country.

Some people don't take animal abuse seriously, thinking it's only an animal. Many child abusers and serial killers start their downward spiral by abusing animals.

We can look at our dogs to clearly see what is wrong with our society. Some people, including theologians, believe dogs don't have a soul. I have heard of many grieving pet owners who have turned to

4

their clergyman and were told dogs don't go to heaven.

I can unequivocally tell you dogs go to heaven. My dogs are in heaven with my loved ones. My psychic has described each dog to me. She describes what they're doing and I know which dog she's talking about because I'm that familiar with their behavior. I encourage you to read the great authors of meta-physical books, and to read about grief and loss. You will find great comfort in knowing our dogs are in Heaven.

It is of interest to mention that a parable, in the modern Bible, focuses on Jesus and the animals. In the parable, Jesus explains to a group of villagers inflicting cruelty on a cat, "Whatever is done to the least of my father's creations is done unto him." I would hope that people realize that pets are a gift from God. It is the best possible gift the Universe could grant us here on earth. Pets give us a perfect unadulterated love and it is the kind of love that we will have in the Afterlife.

The love in the Afterlife is like the love our dogs give us. The love we receive from our dogs is what we must strive for here on earth. It sounds so simple, but yet mankind has not achieved this level of unconditional love and non-judgment. Simplicity is difficult to achieve. Why can dogs achieve it? I suggest we observe them, appreciate them, respect them, cherish, them, and learn from them.

My memories and stories of my dogs may appear too simple, nothing significant. I beg to differ. I am able to love and learn from my dogs. This has brought me to a new level of spirituality. My dogs fulfilled voids in my life and still do. When I lost two dogs at twelve and thirteen within five weeks of each other, I was brought to my knees. I was devastated. I had already read books on grief and loss when my mother died so I reached for more meta-physics books when my dogs died. I devoured spiritual books one after another.

I reached to my psychic who could see my dogs and describe them and tell me what they were doing. My psychic asked me if my new dog Gabbie ever acted like she had an imaginary playmate. I said, "Well yes, every night at nine o'clock Gabbie gets very excited running up and down the hallway. She acts like someone is chasing her." Gabbie always had a toy in her mouth and acted as if someone was trying to get it. She would be out of breath and she'd keep looking behind her. My psychic said my beloved Max and Melody loved to tease her and chase her. I became very aware of their spirits around me.

When Gunther died at only five months old he frequently came to visit. He makes it extremely obvious when he appears. Not long after his death I got up one morning and let Gabbie outside. I walked back to the bedroom to make the bed. Taking a closer look I saw something on my pillow. I could see that a purple petunia petal was on my pillow. I knew Gunther put it there because I planted purple petunias the day he died. Gunther had great fun digging the holes. He dug more holes than I had petunias. When he died his little holes remained so I bought more purple petunias and planted them in the holes. I knew he was beside me as I planted them.

Gunther had lined up three of his toys on the hearth of the fireplace the day he died. I left them there. About two weeks after he died, I noticed when Gabbie and I came home one day the toys had been knocked over and moved off the hearth. I knew Gunther was saying hello. I lined the toys back up the way he had left them. Again, the toys would be knocked over. It made me smile, knowing he was close by.

When Gunther passed on I was distraught. I had never lost a dog so young. I called my psychic and she said he had a defective heart. She surprised me by telling me Max was getting ready to reincarnate in a few weeks. I knew my breeder was going to have some litters in June so I called her and asked the name of the mothers and the dates they would whelp. With that information, I told my psychic. She said Max's mother would be "Norma Jean" and he would be born on June 2nd.

I was happy and surprised Max was coming back, but I was still grief stricken over Gunther. One just can't turn emotions on and off. I had to grieve for the little puppy, Gunther, who had touched my life and Gabbie's for such a short time. When a few weeks went by I knew I had to start responding to the enormity of Max coming back. I knew this was a loving gift from the Universe and my loved ones.

I believed Max's reincarnation was symbolic of a new better fulfilled life and one of a spiritual awakening for me. I knew the Universe and my loved ones were showing me love and support by sending my beloved dog back. They were validating my life and my work and telling me my dreams would transpire at the right time, and that all things are possible. Max reincarnating was a message of love and hope. The Universe was congratulating me on my spiritual understanding. To me, Max coming back was profound.

The following is what I wrote the day before Max was reborn.

"My dear Maxwell. It is Monday June first the day before you're due to be born."

"I am so excited and have a very strong feeling you're already born, or your mother Norma Jean is in labor. Max, I don't know how I can wait to hold you in my arms and look into your eyes once again. Your new body will be healthy, and you will have a carefree, happy life. I know your loving return to me is symbolic of a new healthy, happy, and prosperous beginning for us."

"Max, my heart light, heart gift, heaven sent. Oh, we will have a wonderful life. You already know Gabbie, you will both have so much fun. We will be happy. I love you Max."

I called my breeder the evening of June 2nd and she told me a litter of five puppies had been born. There were two females and 3 males. I knew Max was returning as a male so the breeder described the males. One was shiny black, a bit larger than the others, and had a white vertical stripe on his chest. Intuitively, I knew that was Max. The breeder told me I could see the puppies.

After a nine hour drive to the breeder I saw him when he was a week old. The puppies eyes were till closed and they couldn't walk yet. I took one of Max's old toys, a lamb. I put the toy in front of his nose to see if he'd respond and he crawled following the scent until I leaned the lamb on the side of the whelping box where he cuddled next to it and slept. I took him a new stuffed bunny and a little blanket with my scent and left it in the whelping box. I held the nine ounce Max in the palm of my hand and he cried.

I called my psychic when I got home for reassurance that I had chosen the correct puppy. She told me my loved ones were smiling and applauding. This is when my grandmother said he was their heart gift to me.

Again, I was learning from my dog. I know he came back because our bond was that strong. He knew I needed him. He had always been my man of the house. Sometimes I kid Max-Jacob and tell him my loved ones sent him back because he's so naughty. The reincarnation could not have happened if I hadn't evolved to a new level of spiritual awakening from studying meta-physics books.

One evening my telephone rang and it was my breeder calling. She said she had just received a strange phone telephone call from a gentleman asking her unusual questions. He asked if she was located close to a particular town, if she had two litters of puppies, if another litter of six puppies had been born that day, and if the first puppy born that day had been a female. All of his information was accurate and my breeder wondered how he could know those facts. The caller explained that a psychic had given him the information and he was looking for his aunt's dog that reincarnated. He told my breeder the first dog that day was a female and it was his aunt's dog reincarnated.

My breeder was overwhelmed. She was now dealing with two reincarnations. She has been breeding dogs for fifteen years and had never had anyone looking for reincarnated puppies before. I told her that since she had been open to my Max reincarnating, the Universe was using her for the second dog reincarnation. She seemed to understand and dealt with both reincarnations.

The breeder has a website and a guest book for her clients to make comments. She called me a couple days later, upset that the people whose dog reincarnated in one of her litters signed in the guest book. They were pleased she was helping them with their reincarnation. She was fearful she would get a reputation for claiming she had reincarnations, and therefore taking advantage of people. She took her guest book off her website.

I returned to see the puppy at four weeks, doing the nine-hour drive one way. He heard my voice and was standing on his hind legs trying to escape the whelping box while his litter mates slept. I picked him up and he cried, lavishing me with kisses. I couldn't help but cry with him. His mother and father sat with the puppy and I while I held him. I told the puppy I would be back to take him home when he was eight weeks old. It was difficult leaving him, but I know my loved ones were watching over him as well as God and the Angels.

When I went back to get him at eight weeks old he was in a pen with ten other puppies. I heard the puppies jumping and yipping. I wondered if I'd recognize him. As I walked up to the pen, I looked down and there was Max-Jacob sitting in the middle of rowdy puppies looking up at me. When I saw his face I knew he was wondering if I'd recognize him. When our eyes met I broke out in a smile and scooped him into my arms and told him he was going home.

I tucked him in his crate for the long drive home, but he cried and cried until I took him out and put him on my lap. Then he was happy and curled up and slept the whole way.

Having Max back from heaven has been an absolute joy. I look at him and cannot believe he's in a brand new healthy body. Max was a dominant dog when he was here before. He had been the first dog and then we got Melody. Now Gabbie was here first and Max-Jacob is having a difficult time adjusting to her presence. Max-Jacob doesn't want me to pet Gabbie. He nips me when I pet her and tries to push her away. He won't give up and there is a real power struggle going on.

Since my dog reincarnating I have learned just how close my loved ones are in the Afterlife. I have learned so much from losing my parents and dogs. I am greatly comforted by the communication I have with my loved ones through my dedicated psychic.

The next section of this book focuses on the memories of my dogs that have taught me to enjoy simplicity. They taught me to love unconditionally. They have assisted me in understanding the Afterlife and have moved me to a higher awareness and spirituality.

[Max-Jacob cuddled next to his lamb from his previous life.]

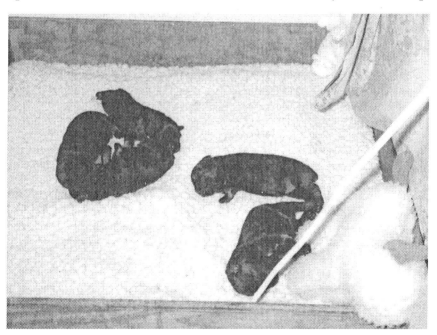

FOR HUMANS
WORDS OF SIMPLICITY

From: My Dog Max and Melody

LOVE

Love for a pet is like the love in the Afterlife.

Love is the light in ones heart when we think of our human.

Love is the pure joy we feel when we're with our human.

A heart-felt kiss is our way of saying, "I love you." No expectations.

Love reaches the stars. It is timeless, pure, authentic, and never ends.

Love is living with the heart.

We teach humans that love is totally unconditional with a devotion and blissful joy that is pure.

Through the love for us, human's learn how to love, and how to receive love.

Love is a new life that unfolds at the perfect time like a beautiful unfolding flower.

Yips of excitement, a lick of the face, a tug at your shoelaces is love.

A sigh, settled for the day, and cuddled next to my human is love.

HAPPINESS

A dog's love for a human, or a human's love for a dog is happiness.

A dog's love for a human is pure. Humans able to appreciate this ideal love will be happy.

Humans need to learn how to love one another by emulating their dog's love for them. Appreciate nature and love for the Universe transpires.

A dog's freedom is the happiness his human has when his faithful friend greets him with yips and kisses.

Happiness is the human's heart light.

Seek happiness in pure simplicity like the pure love dogs have for humans. More happiness will follow, but your dog is constant and sustains you.

Happiness is love, and my human is love.

JOY

Joy is the devoted love dogs feel for their humans. It is the sound of the car, and the sound of the door opening.

Joy is a biscuit right from my human's hands.

A walk with a human on a cold brisk day is joy. Take time to lift your leg and smell the tree for this is the joy of the moment.

Joy is curling up in front of a fireplace while the wind howls.

A bowl of warm food from our human brings us joy.

Joy is our human's touch and kind words.

If dogs want to know and love humans they will encounter some turkeys.

If humans want to know and love their dogs they will experience some accidents on the floor.

PEACE

Peace is being safe asleep beside my human.

A long afternoon nap dreaming of my human's return home.

Peace for a dog flows unobstructed. Humans tend to worry about the future, which prevents peacefulness.

A walk with our human on a spring day, taking time to notice the renewal of life around us.

The sound of our human's voice.

A walk with our human, exploring the mysteries of nature.

DEVOTION

Dog's devotion to their human doesn't die with the body.

The ultimate act of devotion to my human was my reincarnation.

My human's devotion was knowing where to find me when I reincarnated.

Taking care of my human when she is sick.

Devotion is the love for my mistress that will never end.

We love our humans when they are sick, or sad. We don't care how much money they have, what kind of car they drive, or how big their house is.

PLAY

Play with your human when their heart is breaking.

Play keeps your human from being too serious, and puts a smile on their face. A lot of times humans take themselves too seriously and forget to play and smile.

Play is good exercise for your human. Humans don't always take the time to play.

Humans need to learn to play, but most of all they need to learn to relax and enjoy each beautiful moment of every day.

Our humans need to know play is a healthy interaction and doesn't need to be competitive.

Play is pulling your human's flowers out of the garden roots and all and brining them into the house. It makes my human laugh. I love to hear her laugh.

Play is shredding the junk mail for my human.

LOYALTY

The never ending love, trust, and devotion for our human

Our watchful eye for the return of our human.

Protecting our human's home from intruders.

Sleeping on our human's lap.

A human comes first, no matter what happens.

When we adopt a human it's for ever and ever. We never tire of them and leave them along the side of the road.

SIMPLICITY

Lead with your heart, love with your heart. This is simple for a dog who knows simplicity is what's important. Our humans do way too much thinking and rationalizing.

A simple smile warms the heart and activates the spirit.

Do not judge, just love.

Light from the heart lights our way. Our heart light is our heart gift.

Living is being born throughout our life. Earth is life, and the Afterlife is life. We come and go just as the sun rises and the sun sets.

Simplicity in the consistency of nature.

Section Two

HEART LIGHT HEART GIFT

By: Maxwell

My name was Maxwell when I lived my first life of thirteen and a half years. I had a wonderful life with my mistress. She was witty, worldly, and intelligent. My mistress' husband was all right, but he traveled a lot for his job. So, from the beginning, I was the man of the house.

After all, someone had to watch over my mistress and protect her. I took my job seriously and watched her all day long. If I didn't feel like following her from room to room I positioned myself in a central location in the house so I could observe my mistress moving around the house. I also listened to her telephone calls because I understood what she was saying and would know if she was planning on going out of the house, leaving me alone.

Sometimes my mistress took me along in the car when she went out. Still I had to protect her on these trips. If anyone came near the car, I barked. I even barked at the gas station. Other times I had to stay home while my mistress was gone. On these occasions I had to guard the house and keep it safe from intruders.

Not only did I have to be alert for unwanted human visitors, but I had to watch for that big brown truck that often came, and the driver would run up to the front porch and throw a box at our door. If that wasn't bad enough, sometimes a big truck would come and steal our garbage right in front of me.

My job guarding the house was a big responsibility. I also had to look out for squirrels and mice who liked to move into the big attic. One day a big woodpecker pecked a big hole in the house. You can see I had a lot to do at my mistress' home. Of course, throughout all of this patrolling of all windows and all sides of the house I still had to make sure I was sitting in the window, looking sad waiting for my mistress' car to pull into the driveway.

As soon as I saw the car I ran to the door to wait for my mistress. When she came in I would jump up and down on my hind legs lavishing her with kisses while she excitedly squealed, "He kissed me." She really loved my kisses.

One day my mistress asked if I'd like a sister. She put me in the car and we went to see a girl puppy. I thought she would make a nice playmate, and maybe I could train her to help me watch my house and mistress. We took her home and named her Melody. Melody turned out to be an appropriate name because she barked at everything, making a lot of noise.

Melody helped me watch the house, but since she barked all the time I never was sure if there was really danger. Melody took over guarding the outside of the house by going from window to window. Now I was able to watch my mistress more closely inside the house.

The man of the house was all right, and Melody and I also watched for him to come home. He gave us some attention but not like our mistress. When the man came home I had more work because I stayed even closer to my mistress. If the man spoke to her in the wrong tone of voice I pounced at him and growled. I didn't want him to sit too close to my mistress, so I sat between them on the sofa.

When we all went to bed, I was the first one in bed because I shared the pillow with my mistress. I liked to sleep with my whiskers in her face. Melody slept right below me cuddled up to our mistress. We both had our own blankets so we wouldn't get cold.

Everyday, Melody, my mistress, and I took a long walk along the wooded country road where we lived. Melody loved barking at other dogs, birds, squirrels, deer, and sometimes we'd even run across a snake.

One Easter Sunday I got very sick and the man and my mistress took me to my veterinarian. They had to leave me there because I needed surgery the next day. My mistress was very upset and worried about me. I came through the operation fine. When I woke up there were beautiful angels all around my cage, watching over me. I would drift off to sleep and see angels, and dream of going home to my family.

While I was at the vet I was diagnosed with another serious disease, but the angels were all around singing to me. Finally, three days later, my mistress took me home.

My mistress took very good care of me, sleeping next to me.

Everyday I got feeling better and better. One day my mistress dropped me off at the vet and said she had an appointment to have her annual check up at her doctor. She said she'd be back to get me. I was very happy when my mistress returned. That night she got a call from her doctor and I could tell something was wrong.

After the phone call my mistress seemed worried and tired. The man of the house went with my mistress to what they said were appointments.

One day they were gone all day. When they came home my mistress was walking slowing and didn't look beautiful like she usually did. My master made a bed on the sofa so my mistress could lie down. She sure seemed tired. Melody and I got onto the sofa to be close to her.

I noticed the same angels around my mistress that circled me when I was sick. They were kind and beautiful.

Soon, my mistress was up and about. She played the piano and planted flowers. Melody and I went for a walk with our mistress everyday.

Our master left the house one day and never came home again. Melody and I didn't know why, but we did know our mistress was very sad because she cried a lot and didn't sleep well at night.

Melody and I were very worried about our mistress so we were very good dogs. We joined her for walks and rides in the car.

When we were in the house we listened for noises and protected our home. We cuddled close to our mistress. We wanted her to be happy.

We were getting older and didn't feel our best. Our mistress got us a stroller in case we got too tired on our strolls. We took turns riding in the stroller, just happy to be alive and with our faithful friend.

One day Melody got very sick causing the mistress to cry. I heard her call the doctor, and she hung up and said, "Max I'm taking Melody to the vet." I was sad and scared and stayed under the table.

When my mistress came home she didn't have Melody, and she was crying the hardest I ever heard her cry. She picked me up, held me close and told me Melody went to heaven and was with the Angels and grandma and grandpa.

I was sad and missed Melody. I didn't feel like eating anymore. I couldn't eat the same food I used to eat with Melody. I was just too sad. My mistress bought me roasted turkey. I ate a little, but I kept getting weaker and didn't drink enough water. My mistress took me to the doctor to get intravenous fluids.

My body was tired and worn from having Cushings Disease since I was young. One day I had a seizure and my mistress took me to the vet and they decided to send me to the Angels, Melody, and my grandmas and grandpas. My body needed to go, but my spirit wasn't ready to leave my mistress all alone. I heard her cry, "Oh no" when the doctor gave me my injection to put me to sleep so I could travel to Heaven. I was met in Heaven by the angels and my mistress' grandfather and he took me to my grandmother. I was in Heaven with Melody. Melody was happy to see me and licked my ear.

Melody and I and my mistress' loved ones were worried about her. Grandpa took us to visit our mistress often. My mistress knew when we came and talked to us. She was sick with grief.

Our mistress found a puppy to love, but she was still very sad. We often went to visit our mistress and her new puppy. The puppy's name was Gabbie. She played with our toys. We played with Gabbie and teased her and chased her all over the house. It was great fun. Our mistress said, "Hi, Max and Melody I love you," and then she smiled. She knew we were close and loved her.

One day our mistress decided it would be nice for Gabbie to have a puppy to play with so she made arrangements to get one. The breeder had a male puppy born nine days early. His two litter mates died at birth. The mother couldn't take care of the little puppy so the breeder had to feed him goat's milk by bottle. The puppy slept beside her bed so she would hear him when he needed his bottle.

The breeder told our mistress about the little puppy struggling to live. Our mistress knew she wanted that puppy so she could give him a good home. The weekend before Thanksgiving the breeder called and said the puppy was ready for his new home. Our mistress put her dog Gabbie in the car for the nine hour drive. Of course, Melody and I rode along to watch over our mistress. We often left Heaven to be close to our mistress.

She loved the little puppy, who had been named Jake. Our mistress wanted his name to be Gunther so he became Jake-Gunther. Our mistress and her dog Gabbie were very happy to have the puppy in time for Thanksgiving and Christmas. He was their Christmas puppy.

Gabbie and the little dog ran and played all day long. Sometimes they'd take a nap, but not for long. Our mistress put up a Christmas tree and laid presents under it for Gabbie and Jake-Gunther. She was happy for the first time in a long time. Jake-Gunther enlivened the house with his antics. Our mistress took pictures of everything he did. Everything Gunther did seemed cute to her.

One night, a couple months after Christmas, Jake-Gunther just went to sleep in our mistress' arms and never woke up. He died and came to Heaven to be with us. I was very upset to see my mistress who I loved with all my heart distraught and grieving over Jake-Gunther. Gabbie was very sad and grieving. The joy had gone out of their lives once again.

Melody and I visited from Heaven, but our mistress and Gabbie were too sad to notice. It made us very unhappy.

I decided along with the Angels, Melody, my mistress' parents, and grandparents that I needed to reincarnate. My mistress and I had a special bond and she needed me, and so did Gabbie. So it was decided I would leave Heaven and go back to Earth.

My mistress was very distraught and telephoned her psychic to ask why Jake-Gunther died and if he was with all of us. Her psychic told her Jake-Gunther had a defective heart and that is why he died, but he was happy with all of her loved ones. The psychic shocked my mistress when she told her I was coming back in a few months. My mistress was happy, but still heart broken over losing Jake-Gunther. It was difficult for her to grieve and be happy at the same time.

Our mistress' breeder was going to have a couple of litters of puppies in three months. She told our mom mistress the mother's names and the dates they would have their puppies. The psychic told our mistress I would be in "Norma Jean's" litter on June second.

I was born on June second and Norma Jean was my mother. The breeder described the males in the litter and when she said one was bigger, shiny black, and had a vertical stripe on his chest my mistress knew it was me.

So my mistress came to visit when I was just one week old. She brought my old lamb I used to play with and a new stuffed bunny and a blanket for me. When she walked to my whelping box she put my lamb in front of my nose to see if I'd respond. I recognized the scent and crawled following my lamb to the corner of the whelping box. I cuddled up to my lamb and went to sleep. I couldn't walk and my eyes weren't open yet, but I knew my mistress had found me. She picked me up, held me in the palm of her hand and I cried.

My mistress went home, but she came back when I was four weeks old to see me. I heard her voice when she came in and I tried to get out of my whelping box to see her, but she picked me up. She knew I was her Max. She played with my mom and dad and me, and said she'd be back to take me home when I was eight weeks old. I was sad, but I knew I had to stay with my dog mama to get big and strong.

The Angels told me my mistress called her psychic so she could hear what her loved ones had to say. She was worried about how Melody was doing without me. My mistress' grandmother said I was their heart gift to her.

Finally, I was old enough to leave my litter. One day I heard my human mom arrive. All the puppies around me were excited and jumping around. I just sat in the middle watching for her. I wondered if she'd know me because I'd grown so much. My mistress came to my kennel and as she looked down, our eyes met. She smiled and scooped me up in her arms hugging and kissing me and said, "Max you're going home."

I rode the long drive home. I cried continuously until I was taken out of my crate. I spent the trip on my mistress' lap. I was named Jacob.

I have been home now for four months. I am six months old and very handsome. I take care of my mistress. I have to keep her dog Gabbie in line. I'm not used to being number two. Gabbie doesn't seem to understand I was here first. I am jealous when my mistress pets Gabbie so I bite my mistress and she says "No".

I am home where the unconditional love my mistress and I have for each other will live forever. We will one day be in heaven together where love is like the unconditional love I have for my mistress.

MELODY FROM HEAVEN

By: Melody

My name is Melody and I now live a very happy, healthy and peaceful life in Heaven. I lived on Earth with my mistress, master, and then there was Max. Max was the boss and monopolized the household. He got a head start because he was ten months older than I was. It took me awhile, but I did find my place in the house. I lived for twelve and a half years before leaving my family and moving on to Heaven.

When my mistress and Max brought me to live with them I was very little. Max played very rough with me, but I stood up to him. I think I was my master's favorite dog and he gave me a lot of attention when he was home. My mistress was very good to me and loved me a lot, but Max thought our mistress was his alone. I learned Max didn't like to go in the car. However, I loved being in the car with my mistress alone, or with my mistress and master. We lived where it was cold so I loved to lie on the car seat in the sun and sleep. This was my special time with my mistress and master.

My mistress knew I loved stuffed animals and she bought me a lot. I cared for the animals and carried them around the house and took one along for trips in the car.

My very favorite thing was the red wool glove with my mistress' scent on it. I adopted that glove when I was a puppy so I could be close to my mistress when Max was monopolizing her time or her lap. I carried that glove around with my stuffed animals.

I had very very sad eyes that made a sensitive person melt. I knew that and I used that look to get attention and find my own place in the home. I had to compete with Max and work my way into the household. I used sorrowful eyes whenever necessary.

Max was sick a lot and had to go to the doctor often. Sometimes I rode along and waited in the car while Max saw the vet. I think he was a hypochondriac and liked the attention. Max took a lot of medication and again got lots of attention. It was quite disgusting, but I just made myself an important member of the household by taking over some of Max's duties guarding the house.

I was a much better barker. I was louder than Max and I was relentless. I watched for birds, squirrels, chipmunks, deer, neighbors, the garbage truck, and delivery trucks. I stayed alert for our mistress and master to come home while Max napped. When I saw them coming I'd bark and then Max would wake up and run to the door. We both jumped and down giving kisses and competing to see who would give the last kiss.

We checked any bags our mistress brought home for food or toys. If I found toys I ran off with both toys and made Max chase me. Then he'd get mad and bark until our mistress came and gave him his toy. He was such a baby and so domineering. It annoyed Max on the rare occasion that I got to our mistress' lap first. Max would go look out the window and bark. Since I was a well trained guard dog I'd fly off my mistress' lap to see what the threat was. Max, being a sissy, would run back and jump in my place. I'd been had, but being a fearless guard dog I couldn't take a chance of ignoring my duties.

It wasn't easy living with Max, but I did love him and I think he loved me.

My mistress opened a store when Max and I were getting old. Max hated going to the store and stayed home unless my mistress made him go. However, I loved the store and guarding it and my mistress. It got me away from Max's dominant influence, and I felt very important being allowed to go with my mistress everyday. She trusted my ability to guard her and the store. I had turkey everyday for lunch. It was a good life.

One day my master left home and never came back. I missed him a lot because he seemed to think I was special. My mistress was sad and didn't sleep well anymore. Max moved out of the bed because he couldn't stand all her tossing and turning. I slept with my mistress even though I didn't get a lot of sleep with all the movement by my mistress. I know she needed me close.

I would take my mistress for yogurt to the local Dairy Queen. Usually Max stayed home. My mistress and I would share a little yogurt. Then I'd lay next to her on the sofa. Max did help me take care of our mistress.

On my twelfth birthday, I had a little stroke and was diagnosed with congestive heart failure. A couple of months later my kidneys failed. My mistress took very good care of me and we were thankful for everyday we had. I continued to have little strokes until my mistress helped me go to Heaven.

My mistress took my bunny and me for yogurt moments before my last stroke. I lost consciousness. She cried bitterly. My mistress met my doctor early in the morning and sent me to Heaven. I did not suffer because my Spirit left my body. The Angels enveloped me with their light and love and scooped me into their arms and delivered me to my two grandmas and grandpas, and my mistress' first dog Misty. I felt joyful and brand new and bounded into Heaven with my red glove and threw it up in the air. I was in the arms of my grandmas and grandpas.

I wasn't sad because I could still see my mistress. I listened to her as she told my doctor all the cute things I ever did. My mistress was sad and went home and told my brother Max I had gone to Heaven. I knew they still needed me so Grandpa and I decided we'd visit them often.

A couple weeks after I died, Grandpa and I went to visit my mistress and Max. When we got there I shook my body so my collar would jingle. My mistress was in bed and heard my collar jingle, but thought she was imagining it. I jingled my collar again. My mistress went to the living room and didn't see anything. She got back in bed and heard my collar again, but this time she looked out the window to see if there was a dog out there but didn't see one. Later my mistress would find out I had been on her bed with Grandpa. We visited often and my mistress became aware of our presence.

I knew Max would be coming to join me in Heaven. He was not healthy and was grieving for me. My mistress took good care of him, but he came to Heaven five weeks after I died. I was happy to see him, but Max and I were worried about our mistress. She got a new puppy and named her Gabbie, but she was still distraught. Max and I visited often and played with Gabbie. We loved to tease her and take her toys. She'd chase us and we'd chase her.

Max never quite found the joy and peace in Heaven that I did. His body was ready to come to Heaven, but his spirit wasn't ready to leave our mistress. He worried about her and watched her from Heaven. He had always found his comfort in our mistress' arms.

Even though we visited her often Max wanted to physically be there to comfort our mistress. So our grandmas and grandpas and Max and I decided he should go back to Earth to be with our mistress. To be perfectly honest I'm glad Max went back to our mistress because she needs him, and for the first time he's not bossing me around. Now I visit with Misty and Gunther and my mistress' other loved ones. Max doesn't remember us and he barks when we come, like a watch dog. We enjoy teasing him, but we are happy he is happy and making our mistress happy. Max now known as Jacob is home where he belongs for now. One day we'll all be together again.

MISTY MY EASTER PUPPY

My grandfather died after my freshman year in college. Shortly before he died he gave me an English setter puppy. My grandfather had always had English setters. I named the puppy Kim. She was a great source of comfort for me and my family. The puppy was particularly significant because she was the last gift from my grandfather.

Kim escaped from our fenced yard a couple years later and was hit and killed by a car. My whole family was devastated including myself.

My dad and I had not always been real close. Around Easter, just three months after Kim was killed, my dad took me to see a litter of miniature schnauzer puppies.

There were eight six-week-old puppies. They eagerly bounded out of their kennel. One puppy in particular, with the most personality and energy, playfully bounced up to my dad. Dad asked which puppy I wanted, and I said, "The one in your arms." My dad carried her to the car inside his jacket to keep her warm. When we got home Dad carried her into the house to surprise my mother. The dog became part of our family for fourteen and a half years.

MISTY'S LOVE

I was in and out of my parent's home while I was in college. Misty loved my mother, father, and brother, but a dog always seems to know who their master is. As soon as Misty was house-trained, she got to sleep in my bed with me.

When I left to go back to school, Misty got into the back seat of my car and just sat there. I always noticed her and had to take her out of the car and put her back in the house. I was saddened, knowing that she wanted to go with me, although I knew my parents loved her and would take good care of her.

I always told Misty I'd be home the next weekend to see her. I promised Misty that we would one day have our own house with a fenced-in yard. Indeed, she did get her own house and fenced-in yard when I got married. Misty was a faithful companion and loved with all her heart. Loving a dog brings out our gentleness. I felt responsibility and commitment to Misty. As she aged and needed me more I was there for her as her faithful companion.

Misty loved the entire dysfunctional family with her perfect unconditional love. Life was not always pleasant for me, but it was the responsibility and commitment I felt for this little dog that kept me going. She taught me about love and commitment and trust. I realized that there seemingly simple things are the most difficult for humans to achieve. Once we achieve our dog's everlasting qualities it is what sustains us and gives us a rich meaningful life.

MISTY'S DECLINE

When Misty turned fourteen years old, I noticed that she could not see well. She had been deaf since she was eleven. I assumed that she had cataracts. My husband agreed to drive my dog to Chicago to have the cataracts removed by a well-known ophthalmologist. Misty did not have what we suspected but progressive retinal atrophy. Nothing could be done.

Knowing my dog was home alone all day deaf and blind tore at my heart. It was absolutely painful for me to leave her each day. The stress took its toll on my stomach and I had to have medication. My job was a very good management position with a fortune 100 company. I was well respected and had received two promotions within two years. The job was challenging, interesting, and came with excellent pay and benefits. I loved my work and colleagues, but I loved my dog more. With some trepidation I resigned my position.

My husband believed I was neurotic over my dog and didn't understand my commitment and loyalty to Misty. He did not support my decision.

Once I was home with Misty, I realized that there was more than failed hearing and eyesight. I fed her in the morning and late in the afternoon. Misty wouldn't settle down after eating in the morning. She circled the entire house, pacing all day long. Starting in the early afternoon, she sat in front of her dish and stared at it until I fed her. This was very unusual behavior.

Misty's behavior continued for several months and then she started projectile vomiting. The veterinarian tried different medications. Nothing worked. He said to give her baby food which would sustain her. She could keep the baby food down but the liquid food did not satisfy her. She continued to pace all day and then sit in front of her dish. I found her distress agonizing. The veterinarian said that perhaps she had intestinal cancer and a brain tumor. Because of Misty's age, we elected not to have exploratory surgery. The vet decided to try Phenobarbital to keep her from pacing all day. The medication had no effect whatever.

We struggled for two weeks whether we should put Misty to sleep. She had lost a great deal of weight. I got up with Misty at night several times because she wanted to go outside and then be fed.

I realized that if I kept Misty alive any longer, I was doing it for me, not for her. I asked my husband if he could take off work and we would take her to the vet early in the morning to be euthanized. That night I was up several times with Misty and I let her have a jar of baby food every time I got up.

I awoke in the morning, knowing we were planning to take Misty to be put to sleep. Misty was at the foot of the bed and got up and walked up to my arms, looking so very weak and sick and acted as though she knew what was coming. She plopped down in my arms. I hugged her and told her I loved her and was going to end her suffering. I told her she was going to Heaven to be with my grandfather. I knew she understood what I was saying to her.

I got up and fed Misty and let her out. When we arrived at the vet I was sobbing and couldn't go in, so my husband held her while she went to sleep.

I'm not sure many people would have left a good job to stay home with their dog. I have never regretted my decision because it seems like the least I could do for my faithful companion. She taught my family and me all about love. When a dog gets older they need us more, not less. I had to be there for her and I am proud that I was.

BRINGING MAXWELL HOME

On a Saturday before Thanksgiving I went to get our mail at the post office. I was looking for breeder recommendations from the American Kennel Club, and indeed, the envelope was in the mail. I noticed a breeder that had been recommended to me twice before. She had a twelve week old male miniature schnauzer, and I had my heart set on a female.

When I saw the breeder's name recommended again, I wondered if we should call her and, if the puppy was still there we'd drive to Long Island to get him. The breeder still had the puppy and would groom him and have him ready.

She brought the puppy into the room. He was the most masculine and distinctive and handsome schnauzer that I had ever seen. His ears were still taped from being cropped. His masculine body felt different from the female I'd had.

My love for the puppy began. He sat on my lap on the way home. I immediately went out to buy him a sweater, toys, and supplies. His first toy was a baseball bat. We took pictures of the puppy and named him Maxwell at my mother's suggestion. The name seemed to be an appropriate name for him.

This was my husbands and mine first puppy. He brightened our home for the holidays and many holidays after that. My husband bought me this little puppy to help mend my broken heart after losing Misty. A puppy is truly a gift of love that brings nothing but devotion, trust, and love. Watching Maxwell and his whimsical zest for life helped my heart heal and know that he deserved the same love that Misty had gotten. Maxwell was a blessing from the Universe.

MAXWELL'S CONFUSION OVER RELIEVING HIMSELF

I had never had a male puppy and I wasn't sure that he was going to be as good a pet as Misty. Max was twelve weeks old when we got him and, we were not to allow him off our deck until he had his permanent shots at sixteen weeks. He was very confused about relieving himself. I took him out on the deck and he would do his business and I'd say, "Good boy! Good boy!" He was excited that he pleased me. One night I was talking on the telephone and not paying any attention to what Max was doing. He jumped up on the sofa where I was talking. Facing the back of the sofa, he put his front legs up on the sofa cushions and urinated. I heard splattering and looked over. Max was looking at me with his whimsical mischievous expression. He thought that I was going to say, "Good boy." He was surprised when I said, "No." I ran to get cleaning materials and started cleaning. It was a real adjustment having had a mature dog for so long and then having a puppy. I thought there was something wrong with Max because he was a male and that I couldn't let myself get attached to him. I called my mother and told her I was going to have my husband take him back to the breeder. I had his toys and sweater packed. Mother said, "He doesn't know any better. He's just a puppy. He'll be all right. Just give him a chance." I did, and Max was house-trained by Christmas.

I was fearful of committing to another dog and becoming attached emotionally because if I did I would be committed. I took my commitments as seriously as a dogs trust in us and unconditional love.

MAXWELL'S FIRST CHRISTMAS

A couple of weeks before Maxwell's first Christmas, my husband and I decided to go out and do a little Christmas shopping. Our Christmas tree was up, and I had put several gifts that we received around the tree.

Max was still a puppy, and we had him only three weeks. I put him in the kitchen and blocked the entrance into our dining room with a box, foolishly thinking that this would deter him. He sat in the kitchen, watching us leave, and I could visualize a halo over his head. We left for our brief shopping trip.

When we returned, we entered the house to find Max unwrapping the last gift under the tree. There were Christmas wrappings from one end of the room to the other, with our gifts in various states of disarray. My immediate thought was to thank God that Max hadn't pulled over the tree and hurt himself or eaten ornaments. I saw pure joy on Maxwell's face and thought, this is Christmas innocence and joy. I enjoyed his pure delight as much as he did and found his antics great entertainment.

We wrapped his gifts and put them back, knowing Max could unwrap them again on Christmas day.

I found as much joy in his antics as Max had in carrying them out. Our animal friends make the most out of each moment. They don't worry about yesterday or tomorrow. Max didn't care what was inside the boxes or how much it cost. I always strived for the ability find the bliss my dogs do each moment of the day.

MAXWELL AND THE TOILET PAPER

Maxwell was the most mischievous dog I had ever met. From the beginning, he spent his days getting into something new. He usually waited outside the bathroom door while I was showering. I did not see Max when I stepped out of the shower, but I noticed the toilet paper roll unwinding and the paper strewn across the bathroom and into the hall. The paper was unwinding all the way to the front foyer, through the kitchen and into the dining room and then into the living room. There Max was happily unrolling the toilet paper.

Instead of being angry over the mess, I saw the humor in the situation and the joy in Max's eyes. I envied his ability to enjoy the moment and to find his bliss through simplicity. His antics livened our home and taught me so much about the little things in life.

THE FIRST TIME WE LEFT MAX

One of the very few times I ever left Max was five months after we got him, he was only eight months old. We left him with our vet and drove to Washington D.C. for four days. I missed him and worried about him the entire time we were gone.

We picked him up after his three night stay with the veterinarian, and he was ecstatic to see us. He got on my lap and fell asleep. The bonding took a significant step when Max realized that if we left him, we would return to get him and the connection intensified with trust and love. We were a family.

That night Max slept beside us in his bed where I had promised my husband he would stay. I had assured him I would not allow another dog into our bed. I was thrilled to wake up beside our puppy. My husband was awake and said, "Bring him up here." I said, "You know if I bring him into bed, he won't be leaving the bed." My husband said, "It's ok. Just bring him up here." So I reached down and lifted Max up. He rolled over on his back between my husband and me with his head tilted back and his eyes dancing with excitement. I imagined he was thinking, "Wow, this is nice. I have finally graduated into Mama and Papa's big bed." He slept in the bed from then on.

Maxwell learned he could trust his family to return to get him. We learned how rapidly we bond with our pets. It is so important to return the devotion, trust, and unconditional love that our pets give us.

MAX ANSWERS THE TELEPHONE

One evening I went to take a shower. When I got out I could hear Maxwell outside the door, and he seemed to be acting odd and agitated about something.

I followed Max to the living room and could hear a beep-beep-beep. I realized that the telephone was off the hook and dangling off the table. Max had answered the telephone. I assumed someone had called. Later my husband arrived home and said, "I tried to call you about an hour ago. It was like someone answered the telephone, but didn't say anything." I said, "That was Max." He heard the telephone ring while I was in the shower and he answered it. Max gave us many smiles and laughs over his whimsical behavior. There was never a day that went by that I wasn't amused and entertained by my loving little friend. He never failed to make me smile and laugh.

THE DAY MAX AND I BROUGHT MELODY HOME

My husband knew I wanted another female schnauzer so Max would have company if I went back to work. I told him Maxwell's breeder had a female, but I had some trepidation about the responsibility of another dog. My husband called from work and asked, "Have you decided if you're going to get the puppy?" I said I hadn't decided, and he said, "I'll call back in a half hour and I want to know what you've decided." He was pushing me because he wanted me to be happy, so I called the breeder. She still had a fourteen old female puppy. I told her I would be there in a couple hours.

So off Maxwell and I went to get his new playmate twelve months after his birth. I took Max inside because he was to be a part of the decision. I knew this puppy was going to be named Melody. Not only had I wanted to name a dog Melody, but I thought Max and Melody had a nice ring to it. We were shown a beautiful little female, as feminine as Maxwell was masculine. I could tell she and Max had the same lineage because they had a quality look, and their pedigrees confirmed my observation. She had the saddest little eyes I had ever seen. Max had a happier, more whimsical, mischievous look. Max got a little rough and she stood up for herself to let Max know to back off.

I put Melody in the front seat and Max in the back because he was a good rider. We started out and Max couldn't restrain himself. He wanted to hang over the front seat and watch Melody. I knew I couldn't risk his being hurt, so I decided to put the puppy in the back seat with Max. They both sat in the back seat all the way home.

When we arrived home Max decided he wanted to play with what he thought was his new toy. Melody immediately found one of Max's toys. Max tried to take the toy away from her, but she wouldn't let go, and he dragged her across the room. Then they chased each other. Melody would grab his neck, and Max would flip over on his back, making believe she had flipped him over. He was excited, and she was able to stand up for herself from the beginning.

Many years later after Max and Melody had died my psychic asked me which dog liked to grab the neck with the other one flipping over on their back. I told her Melody did the grabbing and Max flipped over. I once again could see my beloved dogs behavior.

MELODY'S ABILITY TO BE IN THE MOMENT

One of the first things that I noticed about Melody was her ability to enjoy life. She put her whole heart into anything that she was doing, whether napping, eating, or playing. When she'd decide to nap, she'd nap where she was. She sometimes fell asleep on her back with her legs spread out in a relaxed state and her head hanging to one side. Once, she fell asleep with her head hanging off of the sofa.

I could not walk Melody until she had her permanent shots. Our first walk was on a beautiful fall day. Melody was joyful and hopped along happy and, every once in a while, she hopped up and tried to grab Max's leash. She was a joy to watch because of her innocence and capacity to enjoy life without any other thought but the moment. I envied her freedom.

We all need to strive to be into the moment, and this is something we can learn from being with out dogs.

THE GLOVE

Melody came to live with us in early October. When it got cold outside, I started wearing my red wool gloves. Melody jumped and tried to take one of my gloves when I took them off. At first I tried to take the glove from her, but she persisted. I let her nap with the glove between her paws and she started bringing the glove to bed and took it in the car when we went out. She wanted her "security glove." It was her favorite thing to play with. She carried the glove for years before it found its way to the bottom of the toy basket because she had accumulated so many stuffed animals that the glove got lost.

Melody just wanted to feel close to me. Now I carry her photographs and have pictures all around the house and an oil painting of Max and Melody. I keep their ashes in their cedar boxes near me with Melody's glove. They were and always will be my family.

My psychic told me Melody bounced into Heaven with my parents and grandparents there to greet her. The psychic asked me, "What's with the glove, she just threw a glove up in the air." I said, "I can't believe you just said that. Melody's favorite thing was my red wool glove she adopted." Melody carried that glove her entire life right along into the Afterlife.

MELODY'S AFFECTION FOR STUFFED ANIMALS

Melody developed an affection for stuffed animals the day she came to our house to live. I had bought Max a stuffed lamb for Easter. He carried the lamb everywhere, even to his dish when he ate. When Melody saw it, she took it, and when Max noticed, he chased her and they played tug of war. This tug of war was hard on the little lamb and he often tore. I sewed him back to new, but this tugging kept happening over and over, so I had to put the lamb away. I was fearful they would ingest the stuffing.

I gave my first miniature schnauzer Misty a stuffed bunny for her fourteenth birthday. Misty was blind and did not play with it. When she died, I put it away for safe keeping. One day when I was cleaning, Melody came in the bedroom and saw the bunny. She wanted the bunny, but I tried to put it back. Melody was persistent. After a little tugging, I let her run out of the room with the bunny and noticed that she was gentle with it and didn't chew on it. Max wanted to take it away from Melody, and there were some tugs of war over it. It held up and Melody carried the bunny around until the night before she died. Two hours before Melody had her last stroke, I said "Do you want to go get yogurt?" This was almost a nightly ritual. She hopped over and grabbed Bunny and then playfully hopped to the door. I am now left with the bunny as well as all of Max and Melody's toys. Melody joyfully lived in the moment right up to her death.

WHEN MELODY WAS SPAYED

Melody was spayed at six months. It was snowing in New York when I dropped her off for her surgery. At noon the veterinarian called and said Melody was ready to go home. I took a blanket to wrap her in to carry her to the car, and she was shaking from the cold. The veterinarian was negligent in sending her home so soon in harsh weather after major surgery. I got her home, carried her into the house, put her in her crate, and covered her with blankets. By dinner I tried to feed her, but she had dry heaves and wouldn't eat. I went out and bought baby food and I fed her teaspoons of food. My husband and I carried her crate up to our bedroom where she slept beside our bed. Soon she wanted to go for a walk when I took Max out. Dogs recover so quickly because they don't complicate their recovery with worry or anxiety.

Melody was learning to bond with us. Through experience she learned she had a committed family to love and nurture her. Melody learned to love and trust us by the love we gave her. I found it inspirational to observe how quickly an animal recovers from an illness or surgery. They don't worry about anything, and fully accept their circumstance, and accept all the care they are given with love and gratitude. The love in their souls assists their rapid recovery.

LEAVING MAX AND MELODY THE FIRST TIME

We left Max and Melody for six nights while we went on vacation. I thought leaving two dogs would make it easier for me. I felt that Max knew me well enough and trusted me enough that he knew I would be back for him. I sensed that Melody, being the second dog, was still finding her place in our home. She had come out of a litter at fourteen weeks and had not been properly socialized with strangers and children.

We took their toys and a blanket and left them with their veterinarian. It was a long six nights for me because I thought of the dogs constantly. The world wasn't right with me when I was separated from my dogs.

After six long nights we picked the dogs up. They were both happy to be in the car and going home and both rode on my lap in the front seat.

They relaxed when we got in the house. Melody found her glove and took a nap with it between her paws.

MELODY'S SLIPPED DISK

One day my husband and I took Max and Melody for a walk. We ran a little to let them release a little energy. Suddenly Melody fell down, crying in pain. We thought perhaps she had stepped on something and checked her feet. We saw nothing and we carried her home. Melody couldn't walk, and she lay on her side crying, holding her front leg up when we got her inside the house. I called the veterinarian, and he said he'd meet us at his office.

The vet thought it was a slipped disk and he put her down on the floor to see if she could walk. He gave her an injection of cortisone and said to bring her back the next morning for x-rays.

In the morning we returned with Melody. She was not allowed to eat or drink because she needed to be anesthetized for her spinal x-rays. We were told she had slipped a disk in her neck. It was either a genetic problem or an injury, the veterinarian couldn't be sure. She had to stay in her crate for a month however, she could come out to drink and eat, and she had to be carried up and down steps. She could walk in the yard just long enough to relieve herself.

Melody had anxiety in the crate, so I sat with her on my lap as much as possible. I stayed in the same room with her except for walking Max. There is nothing like the care for an animal that leads to a trust and bonding. Melody was learning she was our family and we were hers.

MELODY AND MY MOTHER

My mother and father came to visit when we lived in New York. My mother was sixty-five and had osteoporosis and scoliosis of the spine. He bones were very fragile and her spine badly curved. After a hip fracture, she did not walk well and sometimes required a cane.

My dad and I had been taking the dogs for their walks, and my mother felt left out. One day she asked if she could go for a little walk and lead Melody on her leash.

Melody was young, and I knew if she saw another dog or bird or whatever, she would pull on the leash. I told my mother that and she still wanted to try. I gave her the leash while we started out, holding my breath, certain that Melody would lunge at something.

Melody proved me wrong. She realized my mother's limitations. Melody would take a step and then stop and look to see that my mother had taken her step. She did this during the entire walk, making sure that my mother could keep up. I was very proud of Melody's sensitivity. My mother and Melody are in the Afterlife and have a special bond and understanding. They take many long walks together.

MAX AND MELODY'S PLACE IN OUR HOUSE

Max came to us ten months before Melody did. He had his place in our home and wasn't going to give it up and he always took his place in the bed. Melody slept right below him at my waist. I covered them both with their own blankets.

When I watched television, my lap was Max's. Melody usually respected this and lay next to me. When Melody did get to my lap first, Max knew how to get her off. He would go to the dining room window and bark. Melody would leap off of my lap and run to the window, thinking that my husband was coming home. Max would then race up to my lap. Finally, Melody would realize that my husband was not there and come back and lay next to us. Max had recovered his place.

MAX AND MELODY'S WALKS IN THE COUNTRY

We lived on a beautiful country road in Connecticut where the area was always lovely year round. Max and Melody loved all the interesting sights and smells.

Every day we took a forty-five minute walk down our country road, always taking a different route. Max and Melody had a lot of energy and a lot of curiosity. They loved to bark at people, dogs, deer, and birds.

They competed with each other, barking, and each one wanted to be in the lead. Melody's nose was always on the ground, sniffing. Melody was more interested in hunting with her nose sniffing. Max was a very distinguished dog, and I sometimes referred to him as a country gentleman. He carried himself proudly. He bobbed his head when he walked like horses do.

I learned to love those walks as much as my dogs. I enjoyed watching their excitement and pure bliss and how they could get lost in the moment. They weren't thinking of the past or present. The moments with my dogs brought me pure joy and relaxation, and awe for the nature and natural beauty around me. I concentrated on experiencing the world around me through my dogs eyes and emotions. Our animals have such a marvelous capacity for knowing what is important and enjoying life to its fullest.

GARBAGE DAY

Friday was garbage day in West Redding, Connecticut. Our home was set back about a hundred and fifty feet from the road, so there was a very long driveway.

Max and Melody watched for the garbage truck every Friday after they had their breakfast and had been outside. They waited at the dining room window. As soon as they heard the truck coming around the curve in the road, they started barking.

It was quite an event when the big garbage truck backed into the drive-way. The dogs became louder and louder as the truck came closer. When the truck stopped and "garbage man Leon" got out and started throwing our garbage on the truck the dogs got very, very excited, jumping and barking. As the truck pulled away, they barked until it was out of sight.

Max and Melody then aggressively focused on the chipmunks and squirrels for the rest of the day because the garbage truck agitated them to the point they just couldn't calm down. The dogs routine was protecting their home and property, and they took every moment of the day seriously.

MAX AND MELODY AND RAIN AND SNOW

Maxwell did not like rain, even a drop. When we got up in the morning, I opened the door to let Max and Melody outside. Unless it was pouring rain, a happy Melody just bounced out the door. Max on the other hand, stuck his nose out the door to see if he could smell moisture in the air. If it was sunny everything was all right. If it was cloudy or damp Max had to determine if it was safe to go outside.

He put one paw out the door on the deck to check for any sign of wetness. If this checked out and the deck was dry, then and only then, would Max walk outside.

Melody wasn't affected unless it was pouring rain. She didn't care and she had no problems walking through muddy puddles. In fact, she seemed to prefer it. Max never walked through puddles. Dogs have their individual personalities and likes and dislikes just as we do. I always found my dogs behavior entertaining. The dogs never failed to amuse me and put several smiles on my face every day.

MAXWELL AND MELODY'S COUNTRY ROUTINE

We moved to Connecticut when Maxwell was four years old and Melody was three. We had bought a house on two wooded acres and then fenced part of the property so Max and Melody could have some freedom with safety.

The first thing they did every day was go outside in their yard. Next was time for them to eat their breakfast. While they followed their routine, I did my aerobics tapes. Max did not like the strange man on the tape telling me what to do. He barked at the guru Gilad until he decided to calm down and just watch me, very displeased. He laid under the dining room table to keep an eye on my activities.

Melody sat in front of the dining room window watching the chipmunks and squirrels and barked at them. The chipmunks running in and out of their holes aggravated her. Occasionally a deer or two came through the woods which annoyed Melody very much. Things calmed down, and Melody laid on her bed in front of the dining room window, nap, and feel the warm sun. Maxwell took care of the inside of the house by monitoring what I was doing.

If I left the house in the morning, both dogs watched for me out the dining room window. Max could look over the window sill, but Melody was smaller and only her ears showed above the sill. As soon as I pulled in the driveway, Max barked and up jumped Melody, putting her front feet on the window sill so she could see. Then the dogs ran to the kitchen door and waited for me and greeted me with jumps and kisses.

I ate my lunch and did afternoon errands. Max preferred to stay home but, Melody rode along in the car and she curled up in the seat and slept. When we'd get home, Max was in the dining room window waiting for us. As soon as he saw the car, he'd run and wait for us at the kitchen door.

Sometimes on a rainy or snowy afternoon Max and Melody and I took a nap on the sofa. Usually Max cuddled with me with his whole face of whiskers right in my face. Melody usually kept watch while napping in front of the sliding glass door, always mindful that there may be a chipmunk, squirrel, bird, or deer.

Late in the afternoon Melody moved to the den to keep an eye on the neighbor's driveway and alert me when the neighbors came home. Max kept an eye on my activities. I practiced the piano late in the afternoon and he'd curl up close to me and listen. My Melody hated the sound of my piano and, if she came in the room while I was playing, she came over and scratched my legs, trying to persuade me to stop.

Before lunch we took a forty-five minutes walk around our country roads in the beautiful Connecticut countryside. Max and Melody loved our life for the six years that we lived in Connecticut. Our life was simple, but full of love, and the ability to enjoy the moment. My dogs gave me love and emotional stability. My love for my dogs made me happy. It's the kind of pure happiness we will one day have in the Afterlife. This is why our animals are so important. They are here to teach us the important things. They are here to give us a sense of the Afterlife right here on Earth.

THE BEST KISS I EVER RECEIVED

I took Max and Melody to my girlfriend's house on a winter day. It was cold so I put their coats on them and left them in the car while I went in to visit with my friend.

However, I decided to walk around back to the pool area to show off Max's blue coat and matching hat. My friend saw us and came to the door with her camera. I will never forget the heart-felt kiss my Max gave me. I will cherish this picture and that kiss forever.

55

THE GIFT

When I bought a gift for Max and Melody I bought duplicates so they both had their own. Max and Melody were acquiring quite a few toys, including a collection of stuffed animals.

One day before Easter I bought one very adorable Easter Bunny for both of them to share. When Melody saw it, she grabbed it and ran. Max knew I had always bought two of everything for them, so he went over to the shopping bag and looked into it to find his gift. There was nothing in the bag. I felt horrible. The next day I went to get another bunny, and had learned my lesson. Again, Melody took the bunny and ran. Max looked up at me and barked as if to say, tell her it's mine. Even though my dogs had two identical toys they still fought over one of the toys.

MAX'S TRIP TO MAINE

We used to go to Maine at least twice a year to visit with my husband's parents. We always stopped at the Portland Airport because my husband worked for a company that was located there.

When we pulled into the parking lot, there was a Lincoln Continental parked inside the fence. It was clearly not one of the rental cars. Out of curiosity, my husband asked who the car belonged to. He was told that the Secret Service asked to park it there because it belonged to former President Bush, and he would be flying in.

While waiting for my husband, I walked Max and Melody. I was enjoying the fresh air and looking around, when I turned back to the dogs, there Max was lifting his leg on the tires of President Bush's car. Max seemed quite pleased with himself, and I thought perhaps Max was making a political statement.

THE SNAKE

I let Max and Melody outside one September morning. It wasn't unusual for them to bark out of doors. But this day they both seemed close to the house, barking with great intensity. I went out on the deck to see what the problem was. To my amazement there was a black snake about five feet long with its head up and hissing, poised to strike. Max was the closest to me, so I grabbed him and put him indoors. I went back to get Melody, who wouldn't back down from the hissing snake. I moved slowly, with my eyes on the snake and grabbed Melody.

I am petrified of snakes, so I called Animal Control. I was told that it wasn't poisonous. I asked why it was in our yard close to the foundation of the house. I was told that snakes don't see well and it probably crawled toward the foundation of the house, thinking it was rock. Just another day in the Connecticut woods with my fearless dogs.

MAX AND MELODY WATCHING FOR PAPA DOG

Max and Melody's human papa traveled extensively much of the time, and they learned his routine very quickly. If they saw him packing, they knew he was going away. Unless I told them papa dog would be home tonight, they wouldn't watch for him out the dining room window until Friday. Melody stayed at the window even if he didn't get home until late. Max watched until he got tired, and then he'd come and lie on my lap, until he heard Melody bark. Then Max flew off my lap and ran as fast as he could to beat Melody to the back door to greet Papa Dog.

When my husband walked in the door, they'd compete to see which would get the most attention. Repeatedly I told my husband that he had to give them equal time. Sometimes he was tired and didn't want to pet them and he'd ignore their yips of excitement. I said, "Just remember they've been watching and listening for you for hours." I'd ask my husband where else one could find loyal companions like these. So he'd give them the attention they waited for. The love from dogs is genuine and a pleasure to experience. If humans greeted each other with pure love and joy in their hearts you can imagine how much happier and fulfilled our lives would be.

THE NIGHT THE SECURITY ALARM WENT OFF

While we were living in Connecticut, the security alarm went off. My husband was out of town. I was awakened from a sound sleep and it took a few seconds to figure out what I was hearing and process it.

Once I realized what it was, I couldn't believe what I was hearing. My bedroom door was locked, and I quickly put a wing-back chair in front of the door. I thought the security company would be calling any second. They did not call, so I called them. They didn't know my alarm was activated and said, "It is probably malfunctioning." I said, "Probably!" They said, "Do you want us to call the police?" I said, "Yes."

About ten minutes later the police officers rang the bell. I removed my chair from the door, unlocked it and went to open the front door. I had left Max and Melody in the bedroom. The police officers checked the doors for any signs of entry and then went out into the back yard to look around. They came back and said they saw no sign of entry and that the alarm had probably malfunctioned because of the wind. I thanked them, and they left.

I went back to my bedroom and planned to get right into bed. However Max and Melody were too excited. They knew someone had come into the house. So I let them go downstairs to see that the police officers were gone. That didn't satisfy their curiosity. They wanted to go out. I let them out, and they ran around the wraparound deck and down into the yard, following the scent of the officers.

The dogs covered the entire yard and came running back. Max came in the house, having satisfied his concern. Melody started in and then turned around and decided to check things out one more time. She covered our two acres barking and snorting. She was little, but if she had found someone, she would have attacked. She was a fearless little protector and would have died for me.

61

MAX BLOCKED WITH BLADDER STONES ON EASTER SUNDAY

It was a usual Easter Sunday. About mid-morning I realized Max was going outside every five minutes. He was trotting around the yard, lifting his leg every couple of feet. I went outside and at first I thought that it must be a bladder infection, but as it continued, I went out to see if he was passing any urine. He was not.

I called our veterinarian, and he said he'd meet us at his office in half an hour. I carried Max to the car and held him on my lap where he stayed until we got to the vet, who was pulling into the parking lot when we arrived.

The doctor felt Max's bladder and said that it was full. Max was obstructed with bladder stones. The vet had to sedate Max to unblock him and x-ray to see the stones. He said we should leave Max there so he could be stabilized for surgery the next day and that he'd call and give us a report. He'd unblocked the urethra and x-rayed the bladder, and there was a pile of very small stones. We told him to do the surgery.

It was a very tense and stressful Easter Sunday without Maxwell around. I called the veterinarian Monday morning, thinking the surgery should be over. The assistant said that Max was blocked with another stone overnight and the vet was still trying to unblock him before he could do the surgery. He finally called and said that he'd removed the stones, and that Max was resting with some discomfort. If everything progressed normally, Max could go home in two days. I was very confident because Max was a fighter and in good hands.

A year before, Max hadn't been eating in the morning as usual and seemed listless. At first I attributed it to our move to a new house. After about three months I took him to the vet who thought his liver felt small, so he x-rayed. It was half the size that a normal liver should be. He felt that we had to rule out Cirrhosis, cancer, and Cushings Disease. A biopsy was done, and we had to wait one week to find out the fate of our beautiful Maxwell. He tested negative for everything. By process of elimination the radiologist determined that Max must have a liver shunt where the arteries in the liver travel the wrong way, causing the liver to shrink. This wasn't good news. Nothing could be done except to try to retain what was left of Max's liver.

While Max was hospitalized for his bladder surgery I mentioned to the veterinarian that he had a ravenous appetite and had put on weight and that he had been drinking excessively. Even though Max had been checked over a year ago for Cushings Disease and tested negative, the vet thought that we should re-test him with an eight hour blood test. Max was fortunate. He tested positive for Cushings Disease this time which was preferable to diagnosis of a liver shunt. Max had to be given a chemotherapy drug, lysedren, a very potent drug that had to be regulated with blood work, just as if he had diabetes. He would also have to take Prednisone with the lysedren to counteract the side effects of the lysedren. Max was prone to all kinds of infections: bladder, gall bladder, eyes, ears, skin and even his tail. Max also needed to go on a urinary diet prescription dog food formulated to avoid bladder stones.

Max was happy to see me but very uncomfortable. The technician put him in my car, and I noticed the huge scar. The veterinarian said Max would be dribbling blood for a few days. I made him a bed near the heat register in the kitchen, covered him with a blanket, and covered the kitchen floor with papers. The vet said to get him to eat so he'd drink a lot. Melody and I moved to the sofa in the den so I could hear Max. When he got up I'd hear the papers crumpling and get up, but Max couldn't make it to the door to go outside. I'd guide him back to his bed and cover him up and put down fresh papers for the next time. Soon Max could make it all the way outside. I made him a bed on the sofa and sat with him much of the time.

The next week I was having a routine mammography which turned out to be anything but routine. In fact, I almost walked out of the waiting room because my mind was set on picking Max up at the veterinarian.

Late that afternoon my doctor's nurse called and said the doctor wanted to talk to me. I remember thinking there must be something wrong with my blood work because the mammogram was so far from my mind. The mammogram showed micro calcifications in a small cluster. My doctor thought I needed to be seen by a surgeon who would probably want to biopsy. I was panic stricken and called my husband at work. He said, "Oh, it's nothing."

I made an appointment with the surgeon, and the doctor scheduled me for a biopsy. I chose a twilight sleep instead of a general anesthesia. When I woke up I heard the surgeon say "Good. I don't think it's malignant." He told me and then told my husband the good news. The nurse put me in the recovery room and the surgeon said he was going to the hospital to release a patient and he'd get a preliminary pathology report and be back shortly. About a half hour later he returned. I could tell by the look on his face that something was wrong. He walked up to me and held both my hands with tears running down his face. He said he was sorry, but it was a very aggressive form of cancer. My husband and I were stunned. All I could think is that this is one big mistake and if it wasn't, how could I die and leave my husband and dogs? I knew they needed me.

Max and Melody were waiting for me when we got home and could tell something was wrong. I was sleepy and lay down on the sofa. Both dogs jumped up to be with me. All I could think is that I had to try to act normal as possible. Max was still recovering from bladder surgery and had just been diagnosed with Cushings Disease, and his medicine was being regulated. I didn't want to affect his recovery. He was a very sensitive dog and worried about me.

I knew I had to live for my dogs. I did not want them to see me sick and I rejected the idea that I would require chemotherapy or radiation. I just wanted to have the surgery as quickly as possible and resume my normal activities. Max had been an inspiration to watch rapidly recover from bladder surgery. Now he had Cushings Disease and needed more love and care. I didn't want him to worry about me.

I believe the desire to care for my dogs allowed me to get through my ordeal. My Max and Melody now had the opportunity to comfort me two days after my surgery I took them for a walk on the warm spring day. By watching Max get well, I knew I could also get well.

MAX AND MELODY'S MOVE TO CALIFORNIA

When Max was eleven and Melody was ten years old, we moved from the Connecticut country to California, where our new home was on a golf course. This was quite an adjustment because Max and Melody were used to looking outside and barking at squirrels, chipmunks, birds, and deer. Now when they looked outside, they saw people hitting balls and driving golf carts.

When I took them out for a walk, we passed driveway after driveway and saw neighbors. They were used to a Connecticut country road. I am sure they thought all these people were on our property. They'd get especially angry when a golf cart with a dog in it went by.

I opened a retail store and Melody went to the store everyday. Max came when he wanted to, but he preferred to stay home and guard the house. Melody took on the responsibility of guarding my store. For older dogs they adapted to their new environment very well.

I did not know that I would soon face the death of my mother and the beginning of a three year divorce. Max and Melody were instrumental in helping me through this pain with their devotion and love. Because of them I got up each morning and moved throughout the day for them. I did not want them to be anymore stressed than necessary. I wanted them to live out their lives with a sense of normalcy. When Max and Melody both died just years later within five weeks of each other I entered a clinical depression.

Even in death my dogs were there for me. Their spirits visited each night and played with my new puppy Gabbie. They loved to tease her by taking her toys. Gabbie chased them. Spiritually it helped me move to a higher level. I knew the love I continued to receive from my dogs was what life is about. It is all about achieving never ending unconditional love just like what is found in the Afterlife. It is so simple, but yet so difficult to find among people. I had always known that we should look to our dogs to learn from them, but the message these dogs unequivocally brought me was how close they would always be. They were still living with me and still loving me.

HEART FAILURE AND KIDNEY FAILURE

On Melody's twelfth birthday she was full of life. I had no idea that anything was wrong with her. I awoke around midnight to a knocking sound. I saw Melody lying on her side with head hitting the wall. I scooped her up, lay her on my bed, stroked her and talked to her. I was fearful of a small seizure or stroke.

The veterinarian said she had congestive heart failure. He gave me medication and said she could live for quite some time with a good quality of life.

Toward the end of August she started drinking excessively and became bloated significantly. I realized she wasn't going outside to urinate because her kidneys had shut down. I called her veterinarian. He was out of town for the weekend, so I took her to a veterinary emergency clinic nearby. Melody was diagnosed with kidney failure. The veterinarian said he would try to get the kidneys functioning again by giving her fluids for twenty four hours.

I went home to Max and prayed. The veterinarian wanted at least twenty-four hours. When I called him he said her blood work had improved and he'd like to continue with the fluids for another twenty-four hours. I picked Melody up and she didn't eat or urinate when I got her home. I called her own vet, and he said to bring her to his office. He said to leave her to see if they could get her to urinate and eat.

What a joy and blessing when the veterinarian's assistant called and said Melody ate and was urinating. Every time I picked up Melody or Max at the vet over the years it was like a gift from God... like seeing them for the first time.

MELODY'S LAST STROKE

I had left my dogs home rather than taking them to my retail store. When I got home Max and Melody were as happy to see me as I was to see them. I sat down and turned on the television, just glad to be home and off my feet.

I got my craving for yogurt. It was almost a nightly ritual that Melody and I went for yogurt. I said, "Who wants to go for yogurt?" Melody always grabbed one of her toys and hopped to the door. This time she brought Bunny. I let her have some yogurt off my spoon. When we returned I settled down on the sofa. A few minutes later Melody had, what the veterinarian believes was, a stroke. She had been having little strokes for months. Like her other episodes, she started pacing around the living room, very nervous and agitated. I always picked her up to hold her on my lap to comfort her, but she couldn't hold still.

I called the vet and he advised me what medication to administer. He had already given me medication in the event of a stroke. The medication did not help. I called the doctor again, and he told me to give her more. I had a bad feeling because Melody wasn't responding like she usually did. My vet said I could call anytime during the night, and he would meet me at the office.

I wanted to give my dog more time to respond positively. She now lay breathing hard. I knew in my heart things weren't good. I lay on the sofa beside her, giving her time.

By four thirty in the morning she was still breathing hard, and I couldn't get her to walk. I called the doctor again and told him that I thought it was time for her to go. She hadn't improved. He said he'd meet me at his office.

I got to the vets office and was so shocked I wasn't able to cry. I carried Melody to the examining room where she was examined. The veterinarian didn't say anything. He squatted on the floor and listened to me describe her behavior and what had happened. Euthanizing her wasn't easy for him or me. He said, "I can probably bring her out of this." I said, "If I let you do that it will be for me, not her." She had multiple organ failure and had many little strokes during the last few months. I wanted to remember Melody hopping to the door to go get yogurt. The doctor agreed. He left the room and returned to shave her leg where he'd inject her. She was breathing hard. I said, "Melody it's all right to go and grandma will be waiting for you and I love you." Melody was given the injection, and her breathing slowly subsided. She was gone to be with my mother.

I stood stroking her, with tears running down my face, thinking the doctor would take her. He just stayed in the room and again squatted down on the floor. I could tell he was saddened. I started talking, telling him countless stories about Melody's life. He smiled and listened as I continued stroke Melody.

Finally, I realized that my dedicated vet was going to stay there as long as I kept talking, so I said, "Well, I guess I shouldn't keep you any longer." He left the room to give me a moment alone with Melody. I kissed her and told her I loved her. I left the room and the doctor was at the front desk. I said, "You can take her now." He went into the room and when he picked her up he doubled over, crying. I quickly left, sobbing.

I had talked for a half hour while my kind veterinarian listened to puppy stories. Melody had been eulogized and had a funeral. Her own doctor felt and shared the loss with me.

I went home to face Max and tell him Melody wasn't coming home. I missed Melody and still do. She had touched my life, and I will never forget her.

MELODY PASSED TO A LIFE BEYOND

A friend of mine is a well-known psychic and channels. Channeling is the ability to receive messages from life on the Other Side. My psychic had brought me in contact with my deceased grandparents and my mother.

When Melody died at twelve and a half, I was heart-broken and wanted to know what Melody was doing on the Other Side. I imagined her lonely, confused, and scared.

When I carried Melody to the car to take her to the clinic, she was still breathing, but I had a very strong sense that her spirit was already gone.

I called my friend when I got home, and she saw and described seeing Melody bounce over to the other side to my mother. I always called Melody's movements hopping, but bouncing was certainly an accurate description. My psychic said she wouldn't have any more information for about two weeks, but by the end of the first week I was still distraught. I called my friend, and she said she'd try to see if she could get anything. She said, "Well, I see Melody running and playing and your mother and grandfather are there." Then she said, "What's with the glove? She's running and throwing it up in the air." I couldn't believe the accuracy in what she saw. Melody had adopted one of my red gloves when she was about six months old. She took her naps with it between her paws and she played with it, and when we traveled, we packed her treasure. We always said, "Where is Melody's glove?" We were concerned that we'd leave it behind.

My heart was warm knowing Melody was playing with her glove and with my mother and grandparents. I was still lonely, but at least I knew she was happy and I'd see her again. I am told that Melody and Max are around me all the time, but it is painful to not see, touch, or talk to them.

MAXWELL'S RAPID DECLINE

When Melody first died, I couldn't tell if Max was affected at all. He was thirteen and a half years old and had been diagnosed with Cushings Disease at four and a half years. He had been on chemotherapy orally since that time. I knew Max was living on borrowed time and I was very grateful that he was still alive.

When Max was eleven and a half, we were about twenty minutes into our walk when he fell down and kept falling when he tried to get up. I thought he'd had a stroke, so I carried him until a neighbor saw us and gave us a ride home. When we arrived, he could walk again, and didn't act like he had a stroke or was distressed. I decided to wait until the next day to take him to our vet clinic.

The next morning I took him to the doctor who determined that the problem was Max's hips. He had acquired hip dysplasia from the chemotherapy he was on for his Cushings Disease.

Max was unable to walk very far and could no longer keep up with Melody. Max was still happy to see me and ate, but he was not interested in what was going on around him, or going out in the car. He slept under the dining room table only coming out to eat or greet me when I came home. He was so disinterested in activities around him that I called our vet to discuss the situation with him. The doctor thought Max was probably in pain from his hips and prescribed another medication. It didn't seem to help because Max's behavior didn't change. Seeing him like this was painful to the point that I was asking myself if he had any quality of life and if I was keeping him alive for myself.

While I was trying to figure this out, my husband of nineteen years left us and never returned. The bottom had fallen out of my life.

Max rallied to the occasion and seemed to want to comfort me and he found a new meaning to go on. Max once again became the man of the house.

When Melody died, Max's body rapidly became weaker and he

slept more. The first thing I noticed was he wouldn't eat the same food that I fed to him and Melody. I couldn't get him to eat, so I tried baby food, an old standby when my dogs were sick. He wouldn't eat the baby food. I bought him a quarter pound of fresh baked turkey every day and he would eat. He slept more and became weaker. I'd carry him to the car to take him to my store where he'd sleep all day.

When we got home he didn't want to eat. He'd go straight under the dining room table. I'd coax him out and put him on the sofa with me. Having him close was a comfort, and I was hoping to comfort him and give him some stimulation. I was not ready for another puppy, but I was thinking of getting one for Max, hoping it would help him.

Five weeks after Melody died, Max and I started out to my store. I stopped at the grocery store to get him turkey and a muffin. I pulled out of the parking lot onto the road when Max jumped on me and in my face. My car swerved until I got him back into the passenger seat. He was nervous and agitated. I thought maybe he had to relieve himself and decided to stop in a place with grass before I got to the store. I stopped and he relieved himself.

I continued on and when I got close to the store Max became agitated, jumping all over me again. I got him back in the passenger seat and started crying because I knew something was very wrong. I reached for a Kleenex in my bag on the floor. He growled and snapped at me. I called the vet clinic and said I was on my way, that something was wrong with Max.

When I got to the clinic I carried him in his blanket. The staff had a examining room ready. The vet said he thought Max had a seizure and was probably scared and didn't know me. I told him I didn't think Max wanted to live anymore. He agreed because Max had been to the doctor twice in the past week, and didn't have his normal fight.

I told the vet that I thought it was time to let Max go. I said he had no quality of life anymore and got weaker by the day. I knew Max had a tumor on his pituitary gland on the brain which is

Cushings Disease. His prognosis since the diagnosis was that he'd have seizures. I told the doctor to euthanize him.

Max was given an injection to relax him. About ten minutes later Max was still awake on my lap, so he was given another injection to relax him. I knew Max was scared, his body was worn and needed to go, but his spirit wasn't ready. After his second injection, I could feel his spirit leave. Max was then given his final injection. I held his head in my hands while he went to sleep. I was crying and again felt like my life was over.

I called a friend to come over and I stayed stroking Max until she arrived. I combed Max's face and legs, sobbing. Finally my friend came and she drove me home.

The agony of losing these two precious dogs was excruciating. They were my family.

MAXWELL ON THE OTHER SIDE

The day I had to have Maxwell euthanized was different from Melody. Max was conscious and was scared and had a seizure. When I called my psychic she said his spirit fought going. He was traumatized and my grandfather was holding him.

A few days later, Max was being held by my mother. Melody went over and licked Max's ear and it flickered. Mother said Max was sleeping and had to adjust to his surroundings and would be up and about in a couple weeks.

Two weeks later the psychic said she saw three dogs running and playing. She asked which dog likes to jump back and bark, and I said, "That is Max." She said Max threw himself on the floor and rolled over. I said, "That's Max." He's home now with Melody. I was glad they had each other.

GABRIEL (GABBIE)

I sat alone in a hotel room, crying for my lost dogs and my lost marriage. I was there waiting to pick up my new female miniature schnauzer puppy. I felt alone and sorry for myself that I was divorced, had lost my mother, and now my two beloved dogs, Max and Melody. I wrote puppy stories of my lost companions and started to write about the divorce.

A girlfriend called totally distraught because her missing cat's remains had been found by a gardener. She was suicidal, and I tried to calm her down.

I faced the next day with great trepidation since I was alone and fearful of committing myself to another dog. The breeder had told me that the dog was show quality but a bit shy. I thought she would need a special home, so I told the breeder I would take her. I left the hotel to meet my breeder with mixed feelings and sadness, because I was thinking of my loss and grief.

I fell in love with the dog as soon as the breeder showed her to me. I left facing an eight hour drive home and told the pup. "You are going to your new home." After I'd been driving awhile, I looked into the crate beside me and noticed her studying my face. I smiled at her and knew she understood my smile. We started to bond.

We finally reached our home. The puppy had left her litter early in the morning and had been traveling a long time. I wasn't sure what to expect when I put her down in the house. Well, as soon as her feet hit the ground, she was running around the house, checking things out. I took her outside and let her run around in the house, playing with her new toys. She was full of energy and was happy to be out of the crate.

Before we went to bed, I put her outside once again. Then I put her in her crate and got into bed beside her. She cried a little when I turned off the light, and I said, "It's ok." Early in the morning she was crying, so I brought her into my bed and she slept in my arms. I got up and put her out and gave her breakfast. After she ate, she played with her new toys, and I enjoyed watching my new dog, even though my heart ached for Max and Melody.

I wanted to give my new dog a spiritual name. When my little six year old friend Natasha saw my puppy she said, "God sent you a special angel." I decided to name her Gabriel and call her Gabbie.

GABBIE DOES LUNCH

As soon as I arrived home with Gabbie my friends wanted to see her. Two of my dog loving friends met me at an outdoor café. We sat outside and the nine week old and five pound puppy was passed around the table, getting hugs and kisses and talked to. People came out of the restaurant to see her. She got used to a lot of attention and strangers petting her. She loved to get her own glass of chipped ice and then shred a paper napkin.

Three weeks after I brought my dog home, I sold my home and moved out to a hotel for three weeks, waiting to move. I continued to take Gabbie everywhere in her bag, getting her used to traveling. Finally, the time came to move to our new house.

The day I moved into my new home with Gabbie I spiraled down into a worse depression. As I unpacked and found photographs of Max and Melody and their belongings I cried the hardest I'd ever cried in my life. It was absolutely heart wrenching. My new little puppy became very used to seeing and hearing me cry. I felt significant guilt exposing her to my grief, but I had fallen apart.

This precious little puppy put her precious paws around my neck and hugged me with all her heart. She loved to sit and put her paw in my hand actually clutching it. Later on she began licking the tears off my face. I had to keep going for Gabbie. I made a life long commitment to her the day I brought her home. She had no one else but me. We had bonded and I had to take care of her.

GABBIE'S FIRST AIRPLANE RIDE

Gabbie was four months old when I took her on her first flight. I had purchased a soft-sided bag when I brought her home at nine weeks. I knew I should break her into her bag slowly to acclimate her, so I started by putting her in the bag and carrying her into stores to shop. I took her to the dentist and to visit friends. I asked my friend who owns a store if I could leave Gabbie there in her bag while I went for lunch. When I returned two hours later my friend said Gabbie hadn't made a sound, even with customers coming and going.

Finally the day of the flight came. I carried her into the airport in her bag and checked my luggage. I carried her to the gate and held her until the airline personnel started boarding the plane. Once on board, I put her under the seat. She was in the bag five hours by the time our plane was assigned a gate and I rented a car. As soon as I got her in the rental car, I let her out and gave her water. I stopped to walk her and we were on our way.

I had a bad experience with turbulence once and had been a nervous flyer since that time. I was going to Wisconsin to see my father confined to a nursing home. I was also suffering from depression and my nerves were very debilitated. Having Gabbie with me on the flight was such a comfort. She was so calm and loving. There is something about the responsibility of caring for a pet that helps motivate us.

GABBIE AND THE NURSING HOME

I took Gabbie home to Wisconsin, not only because I wanted her to travel with me, but because I wanted my father who was confined to a nursing home to see her and pet her. I knew he would love the dog. My dad gave me my first miniature schnauzer. My parents took care of her a lot until I got married. As soon as my husband and I bought a home, Misty came and lived with us until she died.

Gabbie and I waited for my dad in his room. When Dad came to his room he was surprised to see me. I put Gabbie in his lap and he was so pleased.

Gabbie let Dad hold her as we wheeled him down to the lounge. She knew we were in a serious place and she didn't chew or play. She let him hold her. Seeing Dad and the puppy interacting was special. Holding a pet is therapeutic for people, whether they are confined or not.

My dad and I had always had difficulty in showing each other affection. We learned to show affection through Misty the puppy. Dad gave me one year for Easter. Now my dad was senile and unable to speak, but we were able to communicate our love for each other through an angel named Gabbie.

TRAVELS WITH GABBIE

Since I've had Gabbie, we have traveled much. She is a great traveler and sleeps on her blanket in the front seat of the car. I always have her things on the back seat where she sometimes goes to play. Gabbie has become an enormous comfort to me.

GABBIE TRAVELING THROUGH HER BIRTHPLACE

Gabbie was five months old when my friend invited us to her home in Portland. Since we were staying for a month, I drove from Phoenix to Portland.

Gabbie was born in the Wine Country in Northern California, and I decided I'd like to drive through the town where she was born. When we were close to her birthplace, I opened the windows. We were traveling up a mountain road when Gabbie stuck her head out the window sniffing. She started crying. Gabbie would cry and then end the crying with a woo, woo, woo, and then repeat herself. I believe she found something familiar about the scenery and the scent in the air. I have never seen her do that again.

GABBIE A SPECIAL ANGEL

When my little six year old friend, saw my five pound puppy for the first time, she said, "God sent you a special angel." Everyone who meets Gabbie falls in love with her because she is very delightful and irresistible. Gabbie is sweet, obedient, and very smart. If I'm holding her and we meet someone, she puts both paws out and holds their hands. Everyone says, "Oh, look. She's holding my hands." Gabbie is also a hugger. She wraps both paws around my neck and she also hugs whoever is holding her.

Every time this little angel meets someone she extends her paw and actually clutches their hand while looking them in the eye. It's like she was sent her to touch people's lives.

GABBIE AND HER INVISIBLE FRIENDS

I reached to my psychic often after I lost Max and Melody. I traveled a lot with my new puppy Gabbie. When I noticed that Gabbie became very playful running around the house with her toys every night around the house with her toys every night around nine o'clock. I didn't give it any thought. I just thought it was normal puppy antics.

One day I talked to my psychic on the telephone. I always asked her what she saw Max and Melody doing, and what my parents and grandparents had to say. My psychic asked me if Gabbie ever acted like she had an imaginary playmate. I said, "Well yes, every night around nine o'clock she runs around with her toys like someone is trying to take them away. My psychic said, Max and Melody loved chasing and teasing Gabbie. Consequently, I became very cognizant of Max and Melody's presence. I loved knowing how close they were, but I couldn't see them or touch them and I missed that terribly.

The following was written by my mother, Joyce Vandeveer, when Misty died.

MISTY'S SONG

You are home now and,
I can hug you, but only in my heart,
I can hold you, but only in my heart,
I can pet your beautiful head, but only
in my heart,
My heart cries for you, but you are home to stay,
Never more to part.

MY NEW PUPPY GUNTHER

Gunther was born nine days early. This is significantly early since the gestation period for dogs is sixty-three days. Gunther was only two and a half ounces at birth. He should have been five to nine ounces. Gunther's two siblings died at birth, but young Gunther struggled to live. His mother couldn't provide enough milk to sustain him, so the breeder fed him goat's milk from a bottle every two hours. Gunther slept beside the breeder's bed at night so she could feed him every two hours. He had some bad days struggling to live, but he was a fighter. By five and a half weeks Gunther started eating a solid weaning formula dog food, and still had his bottle of goat's milk.

By six and a half weeks he was three and a half pounds. The breeder had been telling me about this special puppy. He was beautiful, had an endearing personality and was a fighter. I became very interested in him following his progress over the telephone.

Finally, I went to choose my puppy right before Thanksgiving. When I walked in little Gunther was walking around the house. He had no siblings and his mother didn't have enough milk so the breeder was his human mother. She nurtured and spoiled him with all her love. There were two other litters of puppies there, and they liked to pick on Gunther since he was so little. The breeder always kept a watchful eye on him protecting him.

I sat down in the floor to play with Gunther as my dog Gabbie walked around investigating. I asked the breeder to bring out the other puppies so I could decide which one would go home with us. They were larger, and a couple took a liking to me instantly. I was wondering how I was going to decide which puppy to take. However, Gunther the littlest at three and a half pounds held his own. He did not fade into the background. Gunther kept coming to the front of the puppies and putting his little paws up on my leg.

I quickly decided I had to take Gunther. I told the breeder to put the other puppies away that I wanted Gunther. The breeder got Gunther's food and formula out and began instructing me how to prepare his food and how often to feed him. Gunther had been busy playing and was tired. As I learned his feeding instructions Gunther went and crawled up on my purse and went to sleep.

When it was time to leave the breeder carried him to my car with tears in her eyes and put him in his crate. My dog Gabbie rode in the back seat with him until I stopped at McDonald's and she smelled food. Then she came up front to hope for some chicken.

I had a long nine and a half hour drive home and had planned to stop for the night. Both dogs were sleeping and I dreaded unloading the car so I continued on listening to Christmas music on the radio. As I drove I was very peaceful and happy. Little Gunther was our Christmas present, and gave Gabbie and I a happy Christmas.

Gabbie was not yet two years old. She had been through my depression and a nervous breakdown. I got the new puppy for Gabbie to have a playmate, and wanted to liven our home. I wanted Gabbie to have a way to release her energy and distract her from worrying about me.

PUPPY GUNTHER

From the moment Gunther arrived home Gabbie thought he belonged to her. The two dogs played constantly. Gabbie loved to torment Gunther by taking his favorite toy away from him and putting it on the bed knowing he couldn't jump that high to get it. Gunther just bounced over to get another toy. He was a happy little dog, but Gabbie again took his toy and ran. Gunther chased her and then Gabbie got a bit too rough and knocked him over. Gunther was only three and a half pounds and was knocked over many times in a day. He just rolled over on his back and got back up and chased Gabbie. When Gabbie let him catch her he'd growl at her and slap her. Then she'd chase him and the entire scenario started over.

Sometimes both dogs laid in the floor and like to mouth bite each other. They loved to play with each other for hours at a time. Gunther had a very dominant personality and did not like it when he saw me petting Gabbie. He'd come over and bite me until I stopped petting her. If Gunther was on my lap and Gabbie walked over to us and I pet her my little Gunther grabbed my sleeve and pulled my arm away from her. He was a delightful little character with a very big personality for such a little guy.

GABBIE AND GUNTHER GARDENING

Gabbie and Gunther loved to be outside in the sun and fresh air. Gabbie liked to show Gunther how to hunt birds and bugs. One of the first things Gabbie did was lead Gunther into the shrubs and show him around. She showed him there were birds in the bushes and if they went behind the bushes they could flush the birds out. Both dogs came running out of the bushes to see the birds fly away. They were very pleased with their accomplishments.

Gabbie also showed Gunther where to find bugs. She taught him to slap at them and eat them. Gunther especially liked to walk in the flower garden. He loved the feel of the dirt between his paws. He began picking the flowers off the pansies and petunias. Naturally, Gabbie decided to help him. Both dogs enjoyed picking the flowers and running with them, and then dropping them in various places outdoors. This went on for quite a while, and Gunther decided to move to a new level. He started pulling the entire plants out roots and all. Gabbie saw that and thought it looked like great fun so she joined in. They started chasing each other with the plants.

Gabbie ran into the house with her plant and Gunther right behind her. They both had a plant in their mouth and wanted the other ones plant. Plants and dirt flew all the living room carpet. I wasn't in the room and didn't see what was happening. By the time I saw the mess there were six torn up plants in my living room with dirt all over. I couldn't believe the mess. Then both dogs came running in again with more plants.

I went out and looked at my garden, or what was left of it. Then I went and cleaned up the mess while Gabbie and Gunther napped. I always find my dogs youthful antics a bit comical and entertaining.

GUNTHER DIES AT FOUR AND A HALF MONTHS

My last day with Gunther was a warm sunny day. I worked outside planting flowers. Gunther was at my side digging holes for me. I'd place the flowers in the holes Gunther dug. He was very proud and would dig me another hole. When I was finished planting flowers Gunther had left me with several more holes that I didn't have flowers for. I left his holes that he worked so hard on even though I had run out of flowers.

I took Gabbie and Gunther to their favorite place to walk. We did a two mile walk with Gunther holding onto Gabbie's leash as if he were leading her. When Gabbie tried to break from his hold on her leash Gunther jerked on her leash. Sometimes he'd forget about leading Gabbie and just bounce along playfully observing all the new wonders of the world. He was an absolute joy to watch. He was so innocent with his whole life ahead of him.

That night my precious puppy suddenly collapsed and died in my arms. He was dead. His life was snuffed out and he was gone.

I have taken his death very hard because the vet doesn't know why he died. I cannot make any sense out of it. I have never lost a young dog. It hurts and I ask why it happened over and over. I simply do not understand. We don't know a physical cause, and I can't find a spiritual answer. I must accept the fact that I probably will never understand why.

I had left the holes Gunther dug in the garden, so I decided to plant purple petunias in his holes. This way I'd always know where his holes were.

GUNTHER COMES BACK TO VISIT

When Gunther died he left three of his stuffed animals on the fireplace hearth. Beginning a couple weeks after he died Gabbie and I came home and I noticed the stuffed animals had been moved. I put the toys back on the hearth to see if it happened again. Indeed, it continued to happen over and over. Although I was very sad it put a smile on my face and warmth in my heart. Gunther always did things to make it very obvious that he'd been there.

One morning I got out of bed and let Gabbie outside. I walked back to my bedroom to make my bed. As I walked into my room I saw something on my pillow. I thought a bug had crawled onto it. When I got to my pillow I looked closer and there was a purple petal from a petunia. I gasped I was so touched. Gunther had helped me garden by digging holes for me while I planted purple petunias the day he died. Now this little dog returned from Heaven to put a flower petal on my pillow.

About the Author

Lynda Austin was born and raised in Wisconsin. She graduated from the University of Wisconsin with a B.S. degree in 1978. A love for nature, horses, and dogs was influenced by her grandfather who taught her to love and respect animals.

The author has had dogs all her life, but it was not until her first Schnauzer that she realized how much dogs teach humans. There is much to be learned from our faithful companions.

Printed in the United States
43139LVS00003B/302